How to Celebrate Creation

Ian Tarrant

Rector of St Mary's Woodford

GROVE BOOKS LIMITED
RIDLEY HALL RD CAMBRIDGE CB3 9HU

Contents

Note
A longer version of chapter 4 and an appendix with some historical background are available on the Grove Books website www.grovebooks.co.uk (search for 'W238').

Acknowledgments
My thanks to members of St Mary's Woodford,
and members of the Group for the Renewal of Worship,
for their help with this booklet.

First Impression February 2019
ISSN 0144–1728
ISBN 978 1 78827 074 8

Introduction

1

A few miles south of my home, there is a park beside the Thames estuary. The land is a reclaimed industrial site, well planted and cared for, with birds and butterflies. Looking down from the park to the mud revealed at low tide, I see gulls searching for worms and other morsels. But to the left I see the Thames Barrier, damming the estuary to prevent flooding. In recent years the barrier has been raised more often than in the 1980s when it was first built, perhaps due to climate change. So here is nature, tamed and wild, along with signs of humanity's despoiling of the world and our actions to redeem damage done.

The idea that God created everything is fundamental to the Christian faith, but there has recently been a growing recognition of the importance of creation themes in worship. This comes out of a growing urgency in wider society about environmental issues, as well as a concern that Christians recognize humanity's role as stewards of God's creation. The World Council of Churches and others have encouraged churches to have a 'Season of Creation' (also called 'Creationtide' or 'Creation Season') during the month of September. Pope Francis wrote an encyclical, 'On Care for our Common Home' in 2015.[1] Congregations have been encouraged to become eco-congregations, through the work of A Rocha.[2] Harvest services have broadened their concerns from issues of poverty and wealthy to include those of climate change. On the internet there has been an explosion of 'Earth liturgies' and other resources.

Alongside this there is a growing concern to see the work of God in our everyday lives. God is with us in our work and play. The London Institute for Contemporary Christianity has encouraged us to think about 'whole life worship.'[3] This Grove booklet is intended to help anybody planning or leading worship to find useful resources; and also to encourage discerning and thoughtful choices. Each chapter has some questions for reflection—for the reader to consider alone or with others.

For Reflection

- Are there outdoor places where you are aware of God's presence? Do you like to worship in the open air? How does it differ from worship in church?

- Are there places where you notice the positive or negative results of humanity's interaction with nature?

2 We Believe in God Who Created

Our worship as Christians should be based on a biblical understanding of the relationship between God and creation, and on our human place and role within it. Good liturgy, hymnody and teaching will reflect these, but there are some resources, especially on the internet, which have drifted away from Christian and biblical moorings, and what follows should help in evaluating these.

The Sovereignty of God

God created all things, without exception. God is distinct from what he has made, and he made it from nothing, without the help of any other being. We see the involvement of Father, Son and Spirit in the creation: the Father taking the initiative, the Son being the Word at the beginning (John 1), the Spirit being the breath from God that moved over the face of the deep (Gen 1.2).

God sustains his creation. Having made it, God did not step away and leave it to run like a clockwork toy, but God remains intimately involved in keeping it in existence. Paul acknowledges the role of the Son in both creating and sustaining:

He is the image of the invisible God, the firstborn over all creation. For by him all things in heaven and on earth were created, things visible and invisible, whether they are kings, lords, rulers, or powers. All things have been created through him and for him. He himself existed before anything else did, and he holds all things together. (Col 1.15–17) Jesus speaks of the Father caring for lilies of the field, for the birds of the air, and for us human beings who are more valuable to him than sparrows.

God is active in creation. God does not only sustain the existence of his creation, but through the Spirit, God interacts with his creatures. When this is reported in Scripture, the interaction is usually with human beings, but from time to time plants and animals are touched by God.[4]

> When you send forth your spirit, they are created;
> and you renew the face of the ground. (Ps 104.30)

All God's works are to praise him. When we come across the call to all created things to praise God, we might be tempted to think that this is poetic excess on the part of the relevant psalmist or prophet. But perhaps we should take it more literally?

The created order was good, but later spoilt. In the first chapter of Genesis, we are told that God saw all that he had made, and declared that it was good. And yet creation is not as it should be. Much of this results from human sin. However, whether we take the first chapters of Genesis as literal truth or not, we note that the snake was in the garden *before* Eve and Adam sinned. And although much of human suffering has its root in human sin, we cannot dismiss the suffering that we fail to explain in that way. Francis Spufford in *Unapologetic* acknowledges with the psalmist that the universe is 'wonderfully made,' but observes with honesty that it is also 'carelessly, dangerously and clumsily made. And aswarm with cruelties.'[5] Tom Torrance in his book *Divine and Contingent Order* reflects on the fallen-ness of creation which is hard to link to the fallen-ness of humanity: natural disasters such as earthquakes, as well as predatory creatures great and small.[6] Did the evil behind the serpent also infect the unfolding of the natural order? We do not have an easy answer to this. But Scripture tells us of the compassion of God for his suffering creatures, of God's personal engagement with the suffering of humanity through the incarnation, and of the resurrection which proclaims the victory of life over death.

Christ brings redemption to the whole of creation. As human beings, we tend to focus on what Christ did for us, but a broader picture is hinted at in Romans 8, and made explicit in Colossians.

> He is the head of the body, the church; he is the beginning, the firstborn from the dead, so that he might come to have first place in everything. For in him all the fullness of God was pleased to dwell, and through him God was pleased to reconcile to himself all things, whether on earth or in heaven, by making peace through the blood of his cross. (Col 1.18–20)

The ultimate destiny of the creation is in God's hands. Christ is the alpha and the omega, the beginning and the end. The promise of a new heaven and new earth intrigues us with questions of continuity—to what extent will God's new creation bear a resemblance to the spoilt creation which we now inhabit? In the vision of Revelation 21, heaven and earth pass away and are *replaced* with a new heaven and a new earth. However, N T Wright and others argue that other Scriptures promise that the universe we know, groaning as in the pangs of childbirth (Romans 8), will be *transformed* into a new and flawless state.[7] Will our care for this earth be reflected in the new earth? If we make this world a better place, will that contribute to the hoped-for transformation?

While we explore these questions, we remain confident that the Creator knows what he is doing, even if we do not.

The Place and Role of Humanity

Human beings are creatures among others. In Genesis 1 human beings are made after the animals, and in Genesis 2, humans are made before the animals. Neither being first nor being last should tempt us to pride! Humans are told to multiply and fill the earth, but so are the other animals. They and we are all formed from the ground. They and we praise our maker together.

We are made in the image of God and valued by God. Which we do not take to mean that God has hands and feet like ours, but that we have qualities in common with our creator: rationality, liberty and creativity itself. Jesus said that we are worth more than sparrows. In Christian thinking each individual is valuable, and so we are concerned by the plight of the poor and the oppressed.[8] The psalmist says that we have been made little less than God…so what is our role?

Humans are stewards of creation. The term 'dominion' used in Genesis 1 and Psalm 8 (from different Hebrew words, not always translated in the same way) has been seen by some as a licence to exploit creation, but that has not been the historic understanding. In his book, *Creation at Worship*, Christopher Voke writes, '(dominion) need not be consumerist and destructive, but a way of living in which dominion includes elements of subjugation and harmony.'[9] We are accountable to God for how we 'care' for creation. The word 'stewardship' is often used nowadays, but has its own pitfalls—Richard Bauckham in his *Bible and Ecology* details five ways in which we can go wrong when thinking about 'stewardship.'[10] So let us look in more detail at what *right* stewardship might entail, for the planet, and for the animal kingdom.

We till the soil. Adam was told to 'dress and keep' (AV) or 'work and guard' (NRSV) the garden in Genesis 2. The Hebrew words can be translated in different ways, but the essential message seems to be that he was expected to get something from the garden, without spoiling it for the future. We note, however, that after the fall, in Genesis 3, Adam is told that working the soil would become a harder task. Bauckham suggests that in the biblical worldview, 'the land' comprises both the soil and the vegetation that grows in it.

We know and name our fellow animals. The animals were brought before Adam to be named. In the Book of Job, God speaks to Job out of the whirlwind and asks how much he knows about the physical creation, and the behaviours of various animal species. Scientists are still naming newly discovered creatures even today! And as they name them, they describe both their physical characteristics and their behaviours.

We rule the other animals as God rules. God gives us a responsibility to reign over the animal kingdom. If we are made in God's image, and obeying his command, then surely our kingly rule should be as compassionate as his? Bauckham points us to God's example in Psalm 145:

> God is faithful about everything he says and merciful in everything he does. The LORD supports everyone who falls and raises up those who are bowed down.

Do we treat animals this way? Pope Francis observes that rest on the seventh day is meant not only for humans, but also for 'your ox and your donkey.'[11] This is a good place to note that in Genesis 1 God gives humans the plants to eat, but does not sanction the killing and eating of animals. This broadening of the human diet comes only later, after the flood (Gen 9.3).

Human beings are diverse, yet united in Christ Different tribes and nations are frequently listed in Old Testament stories, and in the Babel story diversity of language is God's response to human arrogance. In Acts, however, a special gift of tongues on the day of Pentecost breaks down barriers, and we learn how the early church began to unite Jew and Gentile. In Revelation, all peoples, tribes, nations and languages worship together.

For Reflection

- A vicar once admired a well-kept country garden, and attributed its beauty to God. The gardener responded, 'You should have seen this garden when God had it to himself!' What do gardens tell us about our role in God's creation?

- What practical evidence is there that your congregation is concerned about caring for God's creation? Think about your purchasing; your energy efficiency; your commitment to recycling. As a church are you more or less committed to this than households within the church? Could you do more?

- By what criteria will you select themes and material linked to God's creation? NB you will find it helpful to have these criteria in mind, when you come to look at the resources signposted later in this booklet. Think this through, alone or with others, and make some notes for future reference.

- An enquirer about the Christian faith posed this question in a study group: 'If there is a rational species in another solar system, does it have its own god looking after it?' How would *you* answer?

3 Creation and Creativity in Our Worship

Bearing in mind the doctrinal background in the previous chapter, we turn to the place of creation and creativity in the worship that we offer. Addressing the theme of creation in worship should be more than a matter of having the occasional creation themed service, or even a season of such services. Such an argument is put persuasively forward by Christopher Voke in his book *Creation at Worship*.[12] He writes that getting our relationship right to creation 'in the long term is the most important of any changes that can be made in Christian public worship'.[13] Voke identifies six aspects of corporate worship which give *opportunity* to relate to creation themes:

Praise of the Transcendent Creator
Voke writes, 'Praise, particularly in the opening moments of the service, provides the best place for significant content about the doctrine of creation.'[14] This is not just about hymn content but prayers and readings as well. Alongside the doctrinal and spiritual value in this, there is missional value as it helps outsiders to relate to what is going on. Non-church people often choose creation orientated hymns for weddings and funerals.

Celebration of the Humanity of Christ
Christ in his ordinary human life helps form links with our lives. We are sometimes good at doing this with the suffering of Christ, but there are dimensions to this as well, such as his enjoyment of hospitality and shared meals.

Ecological Penitence
We all fail to do what we could in the area of green issues and regular inclusion of this theme in our confessions can help form our Christian conscience in this area.

The Offering
Many churches use the sentence from 2 Chronicles, 'All things come from you and of your own do we give you.' This could be imaginatively developed on occasion to reflect the offering of our daily lives to God.

Testimony to God in Daily Life
A number of churches have used the 'This Time Tomorrow' approach commended by LICC as a time to affirm that all our Monday to Saturday life matters as much to God as our Sunday times of worship.[15]

Intercessions
Heart-felt ecological, social and personal concerns are brought to God in prayer, 'as the creation groans…and the Spirit intercedes' (Rom 8.18–27).

To Voke's six, we can add three more aspects of our worship:

The Sacraments
In baptism and the Eucharist, elements of the created order take on spiritual significance. Consider this claim by Pope Francis in *Laudato si'*: 'The Eucharist joins heaven and earth; it embraces and penetrates all creation.'

The Venue
In the first centuries of the church, when collective worship relocated from a home setting to a building set aside for worship (whether purpose-built or adapted from other use), it was a matter of course that architecture and ornamentation were used to convey something of the grandeur and beauty of God's creation.[16] The natural materials in our buildings, such as stone and wood and flowers, speak of the inanimate and living aspects of creation. Mosaics, paintings, banners, decorated robes, projected images and so on, can also point the minds of the congregation towards the created orders. For further discussion of this, see chapter A4 in *Reimagining Worship*.[17]

If like most congregations, you normally worship indoors, then consider going outside occasionally! Take care to think through the practicalities such as seeing and hearing, the mobility-impaired, seating, and the supervision of children.[18]

Human Creativity
What better way to honour God's act of creation than by using our own creativity? Church members can write, compose, draw, paint, sew, or build contributions to the congregation's worship. In the resource section of this booklet there is material to help churches celebrate the wide range of cultures around the world, as well as the diversity of human personality with which we are all familiar in our homes and churches. For more reflection on creativity, see section A3 of *Reimagining Worship*.

Let us not miss opportunities in popular culture, such as songs and films that your congregation already know, but which resonate with the message you want to communicate. For example:

- songs such as *It's a Wonderful World* (Louis Armstrong), *Big Yellow Taxi* (Joni Mitchell), *Earth Song* (Michael Jackson—see the official video), *Wake Up America* (Miley Cyrus);

- movies such as *Erin Brokovich, An Inconvenient Truth, Moana, Pocahontas, Avatar.*

For Reflection

- In how many of the nine aspects listed above does *your* worship relate to creation?

- Look with fresh eyes at your worship venue—or invite somebody from outside your own congregation to do so. Does it reflect the beauty of God's creation in any way? Is it well maintained, clean and tidy? Are there any 'quick fixes' by which you could improve it in the coming month? Do you also need a long term maintenance strategy?

- When did you last 'create' something new, in any context?

- Does your congregation's worship ever include something 'home made'?

- Does your worship ever make use of cultural material from the secular world, like pop songs and movies? What might you use?

Creation in Church of England Liturgies

4

Before looking at external resources available for the creation season, it is worth looking at to what extent the Church of England's *Book of Common Prayer* and *Common Worship* material mention or celebrate God's act of creation.

Three common texts remind us of God as creator: the Lord's prayer ('Our Father'), and the Gloria said at the end of Psalms and Canticles ('As it was in the beginning…') both *imply* that God is creator; while of course the Creeds make an *explicit* statement. In what follows, similar distinctions could be made between texts, but we shall not go into such detail.

The Book of Common Prayer

The order for *Morning Prayer* is where we find the greatest number of creation references. Here the first canticle is the *Venite* (Psalm 95), set for every Sunday (except Easter Day), which asserts, 'the sea is his, and he made it: and his hands prepared the dry land.' One of two options for the second canticle is the *Benedicite*, which calls on all of creation to bless the Lord and 'magnify him for ever.' One of two options for the third canticle is the *Jubilate*, where we recall that 'it is he that hath made us and not we ourselves.'

By contrast, the order for *Evening Prayer* is devoid of creation references, other than the three common texts mentioned above. And the order for *Holy Communion* adds no further allusions to the creation, except in the confession where God is said to be the 'Maker of all things.' It is interesting to note then, that the BCP Sunday service used *least* in the contemporary church, is the one which has the *most* links to God as creator; not that this is an argument for the wholesale re-introduction of Matins up and down the land! But a reminder that in losing BCP *Morning Prayer*, some valuable theology became less evident.

The BCP General Thanksgiving, which can be used at any service, includes the words: 'We bless thee for our creation, preservation, and all the blessings of this life…' And we should not forget the prayers *For Rain* and *For Fair Weather*, though these are rarely used in public worship today.

However, in the Sunday and festival Collects there are very few references to God as Creator. The collect for Ash Wednesday, to be read every day in Lent, is addressed to God, 'who hatest nothing that thou hast made'; and the Good Friday prayer for 'Jews, Turks, Infidels, and Hereticks,' although much-criticized, begins with the same comforting assurance of God's love. The collect for the Eighth Sunday after Trinity addresses God, 'whose never-failing providence ordereth all things both in heaven and earth.'

Common Worship[19]

The Sunday and festival collects alone in *Common Worship* yield richer pickings, with about one in six making reference to creation in some way. The Additional Collects score slightly less; and the post-communion prayers less still, with only five references to creation.[20] In the *Common Worship* lectionary, the second Sunday before Lent has a creation theme, and the collects and post-communion pick this up clearly. The second Sunday before Advent has a 'last things' theme, and the additional collect for this Sunday expresses the hope that 'all creation will one day be healed in Jesus Christ our Lord.' You may want to use these prayers at other times in the year when you have a creation focus.

In the Common Worship regime, *Morning Prayer* and *Evening Prayer* are but special examples of *A Service of the Word*, and there is great freedom for choosing material to use within that framework, so it is not fair to try and compare the CW provision for these services with that in the BCP.

The order for Holy Communion, however, is more tightly prescribed, so comparison is valid, and it is easy to find more references to creation in CW than in the BCP. For brevity, we look here only at the unalloyed text of *Order One*. References to God's act of creation are found in the Eucharistic Prayers:

- Prayer A: 'through him you have created all things from the beginning'
- Prayer B: 'though whom you have created all things'
- Prayer D: 'all creation worships you'
- Prayer E: 'you made the world and you love your creation'
- Prayer F: 'by the breath of your mouth, you have spoken your word, and all things have come into being.'
- Prayer G: 'From the beginning you have created all things' and 'that eternal splendour for which you have created us.'
- Prayer H: 'Father, Lord of all creation, in your love you made us for yourself.'

In summary, all eight prayers at least nod at the theme of creation, with the exception of prayer C, the one directly derived from the BCP. For those with the ears to hear, prayer F hints at the involvement of all three persons of the Trinity, with 'breath' pointing to the Spirit (Gen 1.2, if you choose your translation!) and 'word' pointing to the Son (John 1.1).

The Resource Section of *New Patterns for Worship* has suitable materials under the heading 'God in creation.' This heading has items in the following Resource sections:

- Invitations to Confession B6
- Confessions B42, B53
- Kyrie Confessions B56
- Canticles (3 versions of the *Benedicite*) D29, D30, D31
- Responsive Forms of Intercession F47, F48, F49
- Praise Responses G25, G26
- Thanksgivings G61, G62, G63, G66
- Short Prefaces G89
- Closing Prayers J10
- Blessings J69, J70

There is also a fully worked-out service 'All Creation Worships' on page 158.

The *Common Worship: Times and Seasons* volume, in its section on the Agricultural Year, has a sub-section on 'Creation' as well as materials for Plough Sunday, Rogationtide and Harvest. The bank of creation material here overlaps with, but is not the same as, the material in *New Patterns for Worship*. We find:

- penitential material A1–B3
- a gospel acclamation G1
- a form of intercession H1
- an introduction to the peace J1
- two prayers at the preparation of the table K1, K2
- three prefaces (two short, one extended) L1, L2, M1
- blessings, acclamations and short passages of Scripture P1–S4

Much of the rest of the material in the Agricultural Year section could also be used when your worship has a creation theme—it is worth taking a look at.

For Reflection

- Is it better to remind worshippers of creation themes every week, or to focus on those themes in a particular season? Or should we do both?

- Take a look at the material listed above in *New Patterns for Worship*. Have you ever incorporated these texts in your worship? Could you do so in the future?

- Look up one of Jeremy Cline's re-dubbed collects (at latequartet. blogspot.com), and compare it with the original.

5 A World of Resources

Books on this topic are being published every year, and internet searches for liturgical material yield abundant material. Even if it were possible to index them all here, the list would soon go out of date. This chapter is intended to give an idea of the range of approaches which are being tried in churches around the world, and some pointers that might be helpful.

At the end of chapter two you were invited to consider criteria by which you evaluate the material you will use. Did you make a note of what you decided?

Liturgies from some other provinces of the Anglican Communion give fresh ideas and new turns of phrase. See, for example, the *Thanksgiving for creation and redemption*[21] in the *New Zealand Prayer Book* of 1989 (available online at anglicanprayerbook.nz), or Eucharistic Prayer C in the 1979 *Book of Common Prayer* of the Episcopal Church across the Atlantic (www.episcopalchurch. org/book-common-prayer).

> At your command all things came to be: the vast expanse of interstellar space, galaxies, suns, the planets in their courses, and this fragile earth, our island home.
> **By your will they were created and have their being.**
>
> From the primal elements you brought forth the human race, and blessed us with memory, reason, and skill. You made us the rulers of creation. But we turned against you, and betrayed your trust; and we turned against one another.
> **Have mercy, Lord, for we are sinners in your sight.**

The Anglican Church of Kenya has, in its 2002 book *Our Modern Services*, two full services: *Thanksgiving after harvest* and *A litany for the preservation of the environment*. In addition, the order for *Morning worship* includes an optional blessing of the land and creatures in it, 'which may be said outside the church, with the minister stretching out his hand towards the fields etc.'

Liturgies from other Christian denominations will prove fruitful; and there is plenty of 'unofficial' literature from Christians of all backgrounds. One resource book which does not disappoint is Chris Polhill's *A Heart for Creation*.[22] Prayers, stories, poems, dialogues and challenges from a wide range of sources stand alongside writing of her own. One part of the collection comprises resources for a six-week challenge, originally suggested for use in Lent, but which could be used also at another point in the year, with these themes: waste, consumer choice, energy, transport, water and biodiversity.

An appendix to the book offers *A lectionary for creation time* prepared by David Osborne and used in his parishes in the Diocese of Bath and Wells. There are readings (Old Testament, Psalm, Epistle, Gospel) for five Sundays each in years A, B and C. The gospel readings have these themes:

	Year A	Year B	Year C
1	Jesus stills the storm	Parable of the sower	The Word in creation
2	Salt and light	Wedding at Cana	The Word made flesh
3	Rich fool	Do not worry	I am the bread of life
4	Feeding 5000	Seed parables	Treasure in heaven
5	Healing ten lepers	The centurion's servant	Love your enemies

The Anglican Diocese of Guildford has a wealth of material for download, which includes the details of this lectionary, as well as collects and post-communions, and an order for Holy Communion with some alternative gospel acclamations, intercessions, prefaces and blessings. See www.cofeguildford.org.uk and search for 'creation.'

Another source in Britain is the Christian environmental charity 'A Rocha' which offers twelve (at present) themed resource packs online at arocha.org.uk/resources/environment-resource-packs. These include service orders (adult, all-age, interactive), sermon materials, Bible study notes, suggested songs and hymns, prayers, and materials for children's groups.

Going further afield we find the website seasonofcreation.com by the Uniting Church of Australia. Here we find a three-year plan:

	Year A	Year B	Year C
1	Forest	Earth	Ocean
2	Land	Humanity	Fauna
3	Outback/wilderness	Sky	Storm
4	River	Mountain	Cosmos

If you are disappointed to see only four themes per year, remember that these can be bracketed by Creation Day on or near 1 September, and a celebration of Francis of Assisi, on or near 4 October. In the northern hemisphere, a harvest festival might end the season.

A website with a similar address, seasonofcreation.org is both ecumenical and international. It carries links to material from the World Council of Churches, Anglican and other sources. Six themes are suggested: biodiversity, land, water, climate change, 'simplicity and sustainability,' and stewardship.

> If you want yet another set of themes for a creation season, here is one from Christ Church Cathedral in Indianapolis (www.cccindy.org):
>
> - the stars in their courses
> - the seas and all that is in them
> - this fragile earth
> - our island home
> - all creatures great and small
> - from every people, language and nation
> - stewardship of creation.

The Anglican Church of Southern Africa offers a wide range of resources, including another lectionary, worked out services, and small group materials at www.greenanglicans.org

A few more websites that you might find of interest:

> www.creationtide.com *Church of England Environmental Programme*
> www.oikoumene.org/en/what-we-do/climate-change/time-for-creation *WCC*
> www.letallcreationpraise.org *international and interdenominational site*
> www.webofcreation.org 'Home Of The Green Congregation Program'
> www.germinate.net *Arthur Rank Centre*

Songs and Hymns

It is worth looking at the sections on 'creation' in various hymn books.[23] Many hymns simply rejoice in, and give thanks for, the wonder of God's creation. Such hymns have a great value both because such praise exalts the Creator and also the things we cherish and give thanks for we will want to look after. For example, 'For the beauty of the earth' and 'Jesus is Lord! Creation's voice proclaims it.'

But it is also good to have some hymns that have 'care for creation' made explicit. The book *Hymns of Glory, Songs of Praise* has a section headed 'Our response to God in the stewardship of the earth,' comprising ten hymns.[24] Many more are scattered throughout other collections. Below are two lists of hymns that may be helpful. Many modern hymn writers are starting to address these themes, but there is still a need for more material in 'worship song' style.

Hymns That Have a Particular Concern for Environmental Care[25]

'Above the moon earth rises' (Thomas Troeger) A&M531, CP249
Creation Sings! Each Plant and Tree (Martin Leckebusch)
'Creator God with whom we share' (Christopher Idle)
God in His Love for Us (Fred Pratt Green) HGSP 240, MP832, JP347
'God of all ages and Lord for all time' (Philip Coutts) MP190
God, You Have Given Us Power to Sound (G W Briggs) CP256
God's Is a World of Beauty (John Bell and Graham Maule)
Known Unknowns 27
Isaiah the Prophet Has Written of Old (Joy Patterson) HGSP241
'It's a world of sunshine, a world of rain' (Iain Cunningham) HGSP245
'Let creation bless the Father' (David Mowbray) HTC312
Lord Bring the Day to Pass (Ian Fraser) CP 257, A&M543, HGSP 238
Lord Of All Life and Power (Timothy Dudley-Smith) OCOFOL 411
'Lord of all worlds, we worship and adore you' (C J Ellis) A&M540
'Lord, show us how to live' (Chris Idle)
O Lord of Every Shining Constellation (A F Bayly) CP263, HGSP246,
    HTC314, A&M547
'Thank you God, for water, soil, and air' (Brian Wren)
The Glory of Creation (Denzil Walton) on the Eco-Congregation web site
The God Who Set the Stars in Space (Timothy Dudley-Smith)
'Touch the earth lightly' (Shirley Erena Murray) A&M553, HGSP243
When Your Father Made the World (Ann Conlon) HGSP239
'Where are the voices for the earth?' (Shirley Erena Murray) HGSP244

God in the Everyday

'Creating God, we bring our song of praise' (Jan Berry) A&M535
'Creator God, the world around' (Brian Hoare) A&M536
'Christ be in my waking' (Stuart Townend) A&M606
'From rolling plains to deep, uncharted jungles' (Martin Leckebusch)
Oh, the life of the world (Kathy Galloway) A&M548, HGSP141
The Works of the Lord Are Created in Wisdom (Christopher Idle) A&M551

For Reflection

- Does any of the sets of themes listed above attract you more than the others? Would you prefer to put together your own set?

- Could you write a 'local' *Benedicite* like the one in the *New Zealand Prayer Book,* which references features of creation known to your congregation?

6 New Resources for Your Creation Season

If you are putting together your own 'creation season' you may like to include some of the material offered below: three themes taking a broad view of nature (cosmos, plants, animals), and two that acknowledge the fact that the human race is part of God's creation (culture, personality).

Cosmos—the Heavens and the Earth

Readings that could inform your thinking and/or be used in worship:

Gen 1.1–19—the creation of the cosmos

Job 31.26–27—neither sun nor moon are to be worshipped

Job 38.1–7, 31–33—God questions Job how much he knows about his creation

Psalm 8—awe at the greatness of God, and the position of man

Psalm 121—neither sun nor moon are to be feared

Psalm 148—praise the creator

Matt 2.1–11—the journey of the wise men guided by a star

John 1.1–10—all things created through the Word of God

Col 1.13–20—all things are created and sustained by the Son

Topics for Reflection—the Nature of Creation

The laws of physics which appear to govern the behaviour of the physical world are descriptive of what normally happens, and we give thanks for the degree of consistency and predictability that we encounter in the universe. We want water to boil at the same temperature every day; we want our floor to be solid, and our knives to be sharp.

Scientists love to plot graphs in which the results of repeatable experiments fall on straight lines—and rogue results off the line are discounted as errors. In other words, scientists tend to discount unrepeatable events which do not fit established patterns. While the laws describe what *normally* happens, it makes life simpler to assume that the laws prescribe what must *always* happen.

At one level of understanding, the universe seems to be a mechanism in which the location and movement is predictable from one instant to the next. However, in the twentieth century, quantum mechanics revealed an inherent uncertainty in the measurement of a particle's location and movement; and chaos theory showed that the tiniest variation in the initial conditions of a system can lead to surprisingly different outcomes as time passes. The universe is less predictable than it seems.

Some laws seem to trump other laws—eg the laws of aerodynamics appear to triumph over the law of gravity. Are there spiritual laws which are higher than physical laws?

Topics for Reflection—Our Place and Role
There is an enormous range of scale in the observable universe. The smallest particles are 10^{24} smaller than we are; and the visible universe is 10^{24} times bigger. If we are proud of our size compared with atoms, we should be humbled by the size of galaxies. Does size matter to God?

Are we at the centre? There is a human tendency to assume that we are at the centre of everything, obvious in small children, if less so in adults. However, science puts us at the centre of creation in three ways:

- the universe we can see is expanding at the same rate in all directions, so that the farthest detectable stars are the same distance away in all directions, and so we appear to be at the centre;

- on the scale of sizes mentioned above, we seem to be close to the centre;

- complex computer modelling suggests that certain key quantities, such as the speed of light and the charge on an electron, are finely-tuned so that life as we know it can exist, as though the universe was designed as a home for humanity (this is called the Anthropic Principle; arguments both for and against can be found online).

As human beings learn more about the secrets of the workings of the created world, we gain more power to both destroy and create. How can we be sure this power is not abused, but exercised with responsibility?

Engage the Senses
Images from microscopes and telescopes. Prepare a quiz?

A video from youtube illustrating the different orders of magnitude in the universe such as www.youtube.com/watch?v=jfSNxVqprvM or www.youtube.com/watch?v=Fl6qnZzVRAU (others are also available)

Or you can stand people in a line with cards showing different items in God's creation, each item measuring approximately 1,000,000 times more across than the one before:

- neutrino
- quark
- atom
- bacterium
- human being
- our moon
- our solar system
- our galaxy
- the visible universe

If the people holding the cards are themselves of different sizes and ages you can make the point that neither size nor age matter to God.

Collect
Creator God,
whom wave and particle obey,
teach us to perceive your hand
behind all your works,
to trust in your great power,
and to praise your holy name;
through Jesus Christ your Word.

Introduction to the Peace
The whole of creation has been groaning with the pains of childbirth up to the present time, as we eagerly await our adoption: because Jesus Christ comes to bring us the peace we long for.

Preface
We thank you because the universe in which we live and move and have our being is the work of your hands, every atom and every star fashioned and sustained by your wisdom and power. Nothing was made without your Word, and into your creation came your living Word to redeem us. Therefore with sun, moon and shining stars, and all the hosts of heaven, we praise you, saying...

Prayer after Communion
Creator God,
as you sustain the universe with your power,
you sustain our hearts with your sacrament;
as the cosmos reflects your glory,
so too may our lives shine with your love;
now and evermore.

Plants

Readings that could inform your thinking and/or be used in worship

Gen 1.11–12—the creation of plants
Gen 3.17–19—thorns and thistles
Gen 41.15–36—Pharaoh's dream of plenty and scarcity
Deut 20.19–20—do not destroy fruit trees in war
Psalm 67—the earth has yielded its increase
Psalm 96—let the fields be jubilant…and the trees sing
Psalm 126—those who sow in tears
Isa 55.12–13—the trees of the field shall clap their hands!
Ezek 46.6–12—the trees beside the river flowing from the city gate
Jonah 4—the vine that quickly grew and died
Mark 4.26–32—seed parables
Matt 6.25–30—the lilies of the field
Rev 22.1–3—the tree of life in the new Jerusalem

Topics for Reflection

Plants purify the air that we breathe, making animal life possible.

Plants provide us not only food, but also fibres for clothing, and wood, straw and other materials for construction.

Genesis tells us that God placed the first created humans in a garden. Why do we value gardens? Why do (some) people give their gardens so much care?

How should we understand the trees beside the river in the new Jerusalem?

What should we be doing to help protect the biodiversity of our planet?

How is it that in the same world, we have countries where many people are over-weight, and others where many are under-nourished?

Engage the Senses

Images of diverse plants. Or go outside and look closely at plants.

Grow seeds in a jam jar or flowerpot. Send the congregation (all ages!) home with some to nurture.

Show speeded up video of a plant growing from seed, or the plants in a landscape changing through the seasons of the year.

Show different kinds of fruit and vegetable, plant-based clothing and building materials.

Make some leaf prints.

Collect
Creator God,
you sow seeds of joy, love and hope in our hearts:
water them with your grace,
that they may grow and bear fruit
in our lives and in your church,
for Jesus' sake.

Introduction to the Peace
As the mustard seed grows and makes a home for all kinds of creatures, so shall God's kingdom grow and offer peace to all.

Preface
We thank you, God of all creation, that you have surrounded us with all kinds of plants to supply our needs for food, clothing and shelter, and to delight our eyes with their beauty. You sent your Son to the home of a worker with wood, and on a wooden cross he gave his life that we might have peace with you. Like a seed sprouting from the darkness of the earth, he rose from the tomb, the first-fruits from the dead. We who rejoice in the hope of the resurrection look to heavenly city where the leaves of the trees bring healing to the nations. So with angels and archangels, and the whole of creation, we join the hymn of unending praise...

Prayer after Communion
God our creator, we rejoice that
by your power wheat and vine grow on the land,
by human hands they become bread and wine:
and by your Spirit they become for us spiritual food and drink.
Stir us to share with you in the transformation of the world,
through your Son who makes all things new.

Animals

Readings that could inform your thinking and/or be used in worship

Gen 1.20–26—creation of animals
Psalm 104—creatures in God's care
Job 39—the diversity and wonder of the animal kingdom
Luke 15.3–7—the lost sheep

Topics for Reflection

For many people the presence of living animals in their lives is routine and unquestioned; while for others resident in a sanitized urban environment an encounter with a living, breathing animal is unusual.

Why do people value their pets so much? How intelligent are our 'dumb friends'? Do we consider some animal species 'good' and others 'bad'?

How should we as Christians respond to incidents of animal cruelty? Are (all) zoos and circuses cruel? See resources from, for example, the Anglican Society for the Welfare of Animals, www.aswa.org.uk

Should Christians be vegetarian or vegan?

From time to time God, or one of God's agents, uses animals for spiritual purposes:

- Noah uses a raven and a dove
- Moses and the snake
- Jonah and the whale
- Elijah fed by ravens
- Elisha and the bears
- Daniel and the lions?
- Jesus and the fish bearing a coin
- Jesus and his mount when entering Jerusalem

In the Bible we find spiritual imagery based on animals; just a few examples:

- Jesus as lamb and lion
- Herod as a fox
- Pharisees as vipers
- the Holy Spirit as a dove.

In Revelation chapter four, God is portrayed worshipped by four creatures, resembling a lion, an ox, a human being and an eagle. The same creatures are referred to in the visions in chapters one and ten of Ezekiel. They have been associated with the four gospels, with different aspects of Christ's ministry, and with facets of a disciple's response to God. (An internet search will give you the details.)

Engage the Senses
Bring your pet (or farmyard favourite) to church!

Show images of different species perhaps including

- those that everyone loves (eg kangaroos)
- those that evoke fear or disgust (eg snakes or cockroaches)
- those that are endangered (eg rhinos)

Display / touch / smell / taste (as appropriate) animal products in everyday life, whether as household objects, food, clothing, or cosmetics.

Collect
Good shepherd of the sheep,
keep us and all your creatures
in your tender care
until that time when you make all things new.

Introduction to the Peace
By the grace of God, we look forward to the peace of the new creation, when the wolf shall live with the lamb, and none shall hurt or destroy.

Preface
We thank and praise you that you filled this world with swarms of living creatures that swim or float, crawl or walk, burrow or climb, glide or fly. You set human beings among these creatures, with the abilities to talk and think, to choose and create, to obey or rebel. Despite our abuse of your creation, and our misuse of your gifts, you continue to love and provide for us. In your mercy you sent your Son to bring us home to you; and so we rejoice with the angels in heaven, saying...

Prayer after Communion
Dear God, as you love us,
you love all things great and small;
teach us to love well and pray well,
as we follow your Son,
Jesus Christ our Lord.
or
Jesus, Lion of Judah,
defend us with your great might
in shadow and in sun
and give us courage to do your will
in the cold of the night and the heat of the day.

Human Culture
Readings that could inform your thinking and / or be used in worship

> Gen 11.1–9—the tower of Babel
>
> Lev 20.22–27—the people of God to be separate from other peoples
>
> 1 Kgs 10.1–13—the Queen of Sheba comes to Jerusalem
>
> Dan 1.1–6—Daniel schooled in the ways of Babylon

Isa 56.6–8—a house of prayer for all nations

Zech 8.20–23—the nations will come to Jerusalem

Matt 8.5–13—Jesus commends the faith of a Roman officer, and predicts a multi-national banquet

Acts 2.1–12—Babel reversed at Pentecost

Acts 10.34–35—God impartial, welcoming the obedient from every nation

Acts 17.16–34—Paul engaging with the culture in Athens

Rom 12.2—do not be conformed to this world

Gal 3.28—neither Jew nor Greek in Christ

1 Cor 9.19–23—I have become all things to all people

Rev 7.9—a multitude from every nation, tribe, people and language

Topics for Reflection
The many peoples of the world have different ways of living, reflected in their homes, their clothing, their food, their art etc. Even within the same society, there are different cultures, resulting from differences of heritage or class. Let us rejoice in that diversity!

Are there some aspects of particular cultures that all God's people should admire and emulate? For example the respect for and care of elderly relatives in many cultures.

Are there aspects of particular cultures that Christians should oppose? Such as widow burning, foot binding, child labour, the oppression of minorities.

To what extent are gender roles culturally determined? Do gender stereotypes *describe* what usually happens, or *prescribe* what should happen? What does this say about roles in the home, the workplace and the church?

To what extent, and in what ways, should the church reflect the diverse cultures of all the nations from which disciples come? In its worship? In its organization? In its social life?[26]

Engage the Senses
National costumes.

Food, music and art from around the world.

Christian worship material from other countries; see for example song books from Wild Goose Publications, which often include 'world church' songs.

Make use of people in your congregations who come from, or who have links with other countries.

Collect
Creator God,
you call people of every nation to the radiance of your glory,
open our eyes to see the waiting harvest,
and our lips to tell of your love,
that many will walk in the way of your Son,
our Saviour Jesus Christ.

Introduction to the Peace
Our Lord Jesus Christ came to bring the gift of peace to people of every nation, tribe, and language.

Preface
We give you thanks and praise now and forever with people from east and west, north and south, rejoicing that you bring together your children and make us one in Christ.

Prayer after Communion
Creator God,
we have gathered at your table
as members of one family;
bring us to that banquet in your presence
where saints of every culture
will praise you in many tongues;
through Jesus Christ our Lord.

Human Personality

Readings that might inform your thinking—and could be used in worship

Exod 2.11–15; 3.1–4; 4.10–17; 18.13–26—many faces of Moses: rash, curious, reluctant to speak, over-zealous in service

1 Samuel 16.7—the Lord looks at the heart

Matt 25.14–30; Luke 19.12–27—servants with different personalities

Luke 10.38–42—Martha and Mary, sisters with different priorities

Luke 15.11–32—what different personalities did the two sons have?

John 11.16; 14.5; 20.24–29—sceptical Thomas

Acts 15.36–41—a clash of personalities?

Romans 5.1–5; 12.1–3—does faith change our personalities? NB vocabulary used varies with translation

2 Cor 2.1–4—Paul's anguish and love

Gal 5.22–23—the fruit of the Spirit

Phil 1.3–8—Paul's love and confidence

Topics for Reflection
The inclusion of 'personality' in a series celebrating God's creation may be surprising. Human personality is rarely reflected on, celebrated or prayed about; yet we negotiate other people's personalities (and our own) all day long.

By personality we refer to the preferences exhibited by individuals in their daily lives: Our language has many words to describe the personality traits that we observe, such as curiosity, compassion, conscientiousness and calmness. Various schemes have been developed to describe them systematically. Some of your church members may have been profiled by one of these methods at work.

Are we born with a certain personality? (Is Tuesday's child always 'full of grace'?) Do our personalities change as we grow up, influenced by our environment? Does the fruit of the Holy Spirit make a difference?

Should every team, in work or sport or church, have a balance of different personalities? Can we apply Pauline body theology to this?

What links personality with gender? Are any personality traits the exclusive preserve of but one gender?

Engage the Senses
Explore diverse gifts and personalities of people in the congregation or neighbourhood. Or, to retain a certain detachment, consider the personalities of characters in children's stories.

Collect
Sovereign God,
you created each of your children different,
in body and in mind;
to be instruments in your hand,
may we be tuned and ready (*or* sharp and strong)
for the work you would have us do
in the power of your Spirit,
through Christ our Saviour.

Introduction to the Peace
In all our diversity, we are God's people, precious to him, and redeemed by the cross, to be at peace with him and with one another.

Preface
We thank and praise you because in your creation you have revealed joy and patience; and in your Son you have shown us your compassion and constancy. Though we are countless as grains of sand on a beach, and diverse as snowflakes in a storm, you know and cherish each one of us. Therefore we join our praises with those of the angels, *saying...*

Prayer after Communion
Sovereign God,
we have feasted at your table
to be renewed in your service;
use our hearts and heads and hands
to feed those who still hunger for you;
through Christ our Lord.

For Reflection
- We have given you resources for five topics. Would you have preferred other topics? Why?